HOMETOWN, USA

Michael Cleary

With thanks to the following journals in which these poems first appeared:

The Seattle Review: "My Father's Room" / *Apalachee Quarterly:* "What Heathens Do During Midnight Mass," "The Sunshine State" / *Negative Capability:* "Bewley's Cafe," "January Crossing, Lake Champlain," "My Mother Wonders, What Do I Have to Do Before You Write About Me? Die?" / *Gryphon:* "No Palooka" / *Footwork:* "Kill All the Poets" / *The Laurel Review:* "Rat Town" / *Artemis:* "Burning Dreams on the Sun" / *Blueline:* "John Wayne, Freddy Freihofer, and the Buckskin Mare," "Glens Falls: Twenty-Five Years Later" / *Sunrust:* "After Reading The Great American Marble Book and Reflecting on Life's Lessons Learned at an Early Age in Glens Falls, NY" / *Southern Poetry Review:* "Plastic Flamingos," "Bumper Hopping and the Transmigration of Souls" / *The Cape Rock:* "Hometown Seasons," "Colossus, Wobbling," "Catholic Girls" / *Puerto Del Sol:* "Glens Falls Hill: Paperrouting" / *The Texas Review:* "Aunt Sara on Valentine's Night," "Aunt Sara and the Tattoo," "Aunt Sara and the 4-Letter Word," "Fingers, Fists, Gabriel's Wings," "Sun Down, Key West," "At Mud Lake in the Morning" / *Louisiana Literature:* "Aunt Sara and the Birthday Party" / *Berkeley Poetry Review:* "History Lesson" /

Poems reprinted in anthologies:

"Sun Down, Key West," *Anthology of Magazine Verse & Yearbook of American Poetry,* Monitor Books, 1985.

"Fingers, Fists, Gabriel's Wings," *Toward Solomon's Mountain: The Experience of Disability in Poetry,* Temple University Press, 1986.

"After Reading The Great American Marble Book...," *This Sporting Life,* Milkweed Editions, 1987.

"At Mud Lake in the Morning," *Literature: The Human Experience,* 5th edition, St. Martin's Press, 1989.

I also wish to thank the Florida Division of Cultural Affairs for an Individual Artist Grant which allowed the completion of many poems which appear in this manuscript.

Cover Design
Patricia R. Barnett
PRB * GREGORY Advertising
317 14th Street, Suite 2E
Del Mar, CA 92014

SAN DIEGO POETS PRESS
P.O. Box 8638
La Jolla, CA 92038
Kathleen Iddings, Editor/Publisher

Cover art by Shirley Patton: "View North on Glen St., Glens Falls, NY, in 1955." Signed prints available, Chapman Historical Museum, Glens Falls, NY.

Gratitude is extended to the Crandall Library, Glens Falls, NY, for allowing us to photograph the original *LOOK* photographs.

For Beth and Brian —
The pure wonder of their seasons.

"Glens Falls . . . is 51 miles north of Albany . . . equidistant from New York City, Boston, and Montreal . . . the trading center for an area famous in American history."

— *LOOK*, April 4, 1944

Preface

In 1944, LOOK Magazine published a six-part profile of Glens Falls, New York, under the title, "Hometown, USA." Glens Falls (pop. 19,000) is located on the Hudson River at the foothills of the Adirondacks. Indians called it "The Great Carrying Place," an overland passage linking the northern water route comprised of the St. Lawrence River, Lake Champlain, and Lake George to the Hudson River and the Atlantic.

Historically, Glens Falls has served as a halfway point in several north-south destinations: Montreal and New York City; Lake Champlain and Albany; Ft. William Henry and Ft. Edward; Lake George and the Hudson. The region figures prominently in The French and Indian War and The American Revolution, and appears frequently in the novels of James Fenimore Cooper.

Describing the project as "the most ambitious editorial program any national magazine has ever undertaken in one community," the series began with the following passage:

Far from the bombs, fire and fury of battle, America's villages, towns and cities seem safe from the ravages of war. Yet the Hometowns of U.S. fighting men and women are undergoing deep change — in some places difficult and almost violent, in others subtle and imperceptible — but in all cases, permeating our entire social fabric . . .

Here LOOK begins the story of a typical U.S. Hometown — Glens Falls, New York — as it is today in war, as it will be in the peace to come . . . a story of transition which may well set a pattern for other communities.

In Glens Falls are those elements of life we have come to know as American. Before the Revolution, its founders carved a home out of the wilderness and fought to protect it from Indians. Its pioneers wrested from forest and stream the wood and water power to build industry. Its trade marks are known all over the world. Glens Falls has given to the nation statesmen of international fame. Its sons have fought in every American war. Glens Falls contains in microcosm, every aspect of the American Idea, every potential for achievement of the American Ideal.

— LOOK, April 4, 1944

Contents

ANGELS COME TO EARTH

THE SUNSHINE STATE

EPILOGUE

"Glens Falls' foundations run deep into America's past . . . its people are sure of their faith in America's future."

— *LOOK*, April 4, 1944

— P R O L O G U E —

Glens Falls Hill: Paperrouting

Once upon a time,
buildings were stacked clear to the top:
I'd push my newspaperpiled Schwinn
up the beanstalk sidewalk,
head ducked under the wind,
counting the climb on parking meters.
Twenty-one was The Old Irish Inn
where baggy men wandered the porch
in a restless daze,
waiting for meals served family style.
Thirty-four was The Economy Store
("On the Hill, But on the Level") —
best chinos and desert boots in town.
Paperboys could charge there,
but your father had to sign.
Forty-four and I'd stop counting,
The Sugar Bowl balanced on the crest:
in noisy booths we'd nurse cherry cokes
and junior high pride
and orders of homemade gravy and fries.

*"What is there about an American town that **makes** it American? . . . Glens Falls' boys and girls grow up in much the same manner as do boys and girls in all the nation's Hometowns."*

— *LOOK* April 4, 1944

Hometown Seasons

(For My Sunbelt Children)

Dusk trudged through winter days,
snow softening slate roofs, chimneys,
unclenching with a rumble,
the crack of arctic peaks buckling
as the world shuddered apart.

Fall was lush with ceremonies,
storm windows and cordwood,
yardfuls of fathers
watching patchwork heaps of leaves
blaze, bittersweet.

Summer loafed down sunbeat streets
and dogs rambled where they would
or found the cool of porches,
sprawled beneath metal gliders,
twitching through dreams.

Spring held a hundred seasons,
cat's eyes and steelies in a rawhide sack,
railroad tracks to tightrope anywhere.
Mothers said,
Spring always begins on Saturday,
and it did, every time,
it did.

Colossus, Wobbling

Clams, chicken, sweet potatoes, corn —
A jumble of cheesecloth sacks —
A gang of uncles around a foaming keg —
Washtubs sparkling with Nehis and ice —
More cousins than you could count —

After the last last bite,
we'd paddle out on truck tubes
slick and blubbery as whales.
My father would give in to our shouts;
tug the drawstrings of his floppy trunks;
pound down the dock into a cannonball
crash that sent us slipping, nearly
tipping; nearly afraid.

He could stay down forever,
gliding deep through water-
weeds until the waiting squeezed
up in our throats like the unending
end of a bad dream. Then
the surface burst —
a sudden thrashing splashing
us over the sides as he rose
to a wide-legged spraddle, a Colossus
wobbling against the sky.
Then he heaved, and rocked,
and roared, thumping waves
of beerbelly laughter
all the way to shore.

My Mother Wonders, What Do I Have To Do Before You Write About Me? Die?

I got news for you, Santa Claus is long gone, and no one else in this world gives you something for nothing.
— My Father

If you try, love, sometimes you can get something from nothing much.
— My Mother

1.

This Halloween my father would turn seventy.
Impossible, it seems, twenty years gone.
My oldest sister was married, says she knows better,
says he could be easier somehow with the girls,
but I remember him tense, brown eyes brooding,
his solemn expression defining the word *Father*,
all traces of childishness drawn from his face
by the Depression, then the war, then five kids,
the world turning forever serious, all business,
a lifetime of bosses and worry and work
until Halloween birthdays must have seemed a mockery,
another candycoated something-for-nothing lie
he would never be silly enough to swallow
when every day he faced that masquerade —
salesman suit and salesman grin, hat in hand
to every grocery and beer joint in three counties,
buying drinks all around, kissing ass when he had to,
cracking the same bad jokes in the same sad bars
until he almost forgot how much to hate it.

2.

Years back when I still thought Rte. 9
could take me everywhere I'd ever want to go,
we packed into the Studebaker and headed south
in warm October rain turning leaves to spongy rot,
a musk that hung in the air for days.
At Pepper's Turkey Farm
we walked the rows of noisy sheds,
thousands of turkeys waddling and gobbling
under metal roofs pa-pinging in the rain.
At the back we found the waste heap —

15

a horror of heads and feathers and feet.
My father said forget it, wasn't worth the bother.
But my mother saw it through,
gathering a stack of soggy feathers,
newspaper rags wiping globs of guts and blood.

Then home,
my mother scrubbing at the sink for a week,
paring knife stroking quills til they gleamed,
the clothesline a swarm of dark feathers
that flapped in the breeze like wings.
At night she holed up in the cellar,
me wondering like crazy through the locked door,
the snarl and hum of the sewing machine.

That was a glorious Halloween:
under a full headdress I was Apache proud,
feathers trailing all the way down to my knees.
Warpainted with lipstick streaks,
I was the crown prince among hobgoblins,
whooping and prancing fearsome through the night,

the memory a gift no Christmas can match.

Kill All The Poets

Father, I'm far from home/And I have gone nowhere.
— Theodore Roethke

Because I shushed my son away,
tired of explaining: I was writing . . .
A poem . . . Trying to relive my childhood . . .
To see if the words made any sense . . .
Of the way things were . . . When I was a boy.
Because now as I sit brooding,
memory tracing the unfamiliar figures
in the old snapshot, my father kneeling,
big hands balancing my sister and me,
fat cheeks and caps and Easter outfits
    he's never smiling in the old pictures
    staring dark-eyed through the years
    face tight as anger
    and maybe the poor bastard
    suspected even then
    sensed the shadows striping his face
    marked a life that would end without end
    in a muffled aneurismal pop
    like God snapping fingers
    of calfskin gloves
    snap inside his head
Because as I conjure meanings,
inhaling deep drags for inspiration,
making up the man my father was
from a picture clearer than memory
    he smoked too much, too
    the stale smell of it in the bathroom
    smoke-soaked steam on the mirror
    scraping soap and whiskers
    in dry rasping strokes
    toilet paper dabbed on razor nicks
    a grumpy polka-dotted clown
    in bathrobe and flapping slippers
Because as I sit in grim reflection
trying to create poetry from my life,
my own fatcheeked boy sets off
to careen on training wheels
toward bloody knees and disastrophes,
discover rainboats sailing
in the wake of a thunderbulb sky.
And as he leaves ahead of the slamming door,
warns (proud of his good rememory),
"Don't bother Daddy. He's relieving his childhood."

At Mud Lake In The Morning

Mud Lake, Idaho (AP) 3,000 rabbits were rounded up and clubbed to death Saturday by about 800 men and boys . . . during a rabbit population boom that occurs about every ten years.

At Mud Lake in the morning,
boys squint into the ache of sun
richocheting off fresh snow,
feel the tingle of violence
in their fathers' tense smiles and rough jokes,
sense that this is a big and grownup thing
to be proud and fearful on the edge of a man's world,
waiting for jackrabbits to be driven
under the nervous bats and clubs
they heft and slap into leathered palms
to know the unfamiliar power of pain and death.

Too soon the rabbits come,
a stampede of darting, dodging terror
as men and boys strike clumsily
until they find the fierce and ancient fury
in heavy thuds and hollow cracks
and the rabbits start to go down,
some sudden and still, smaller than alive,
others jerking, scrambling on their sides,
changing snow into a crazy quilt
of scarlet specks and patches of deeper red.

With dusk, deeds grow
bold and large on distant farms
until each boy has vanquished ten times ten
again and then again
in warrior tales told to hearthbound mothers
washing bloody socks and splattered overalls
in their mothers' mothers' kitchens.
Fathers smoke quietly with measured pride
as sisters, hostile and aloof,
retreat into wary corners.

At night, boys wriggle slowly into sleep,
happiness wound tight inside,
wonder at the thrill of wood on bone,
snow soiled with matted fur and bloody bootprints,
wonder where blood goes when the snow melts,
wonder how long ten years will be
and how they can stand the waiting.

After Reading *The Great American Marble Book* And Reflecting On Life's Lessons Learned At An Early Age In Glens Falls, N.Y.

1.

Negotiate

Ring Taw? Ringer?
Boss-Out, Bullseye,
Zulu Golf?

2.

Know the Rules

Dubs and Snoogers.
Eye Drops, Toe-Bombsies.
Monkey Dust.
Knuckle Down, Three-Finger Flat:
No Slipsies or Fudging.
No Scrumpy Knuckles
or Hunching.

3.

Ante Up

Ducks:
Cats Eyes, Candy Stripes,
Peewees, Purees, Smokeys.
Mibs, Milkies, Moonaggies.
Clodknockers. Hoodles. Globollas.
Marididdles.

4.

Seize the Initiative

Shooters:
Boss, Black Beauty,
Kabola, Boulder,
Bumboozer.

5.

Learn from Experience

Playing For Fun
's not worth playing at all.
Don't nothin mean nothin
unless it's For Keeps.

No Palooka

A frown gathers behind my wife's smile
as I open another bottle of wine
and pour out the story of my Uncle Jack
to my wife's friends, sidestepping
vacations and mortgages and children's braces,
wanting them to meet me through a memory.

My penance for being a child
involved the ritual of Saturday visits,
the tedious drive to Schenectady
where hunched in the kitchen corner,
Uncle Jack drank beer from a pewter mug,
horseshoe scar hung on the bridge of his nose,
squashed ears as large as saucers.
My father let me join them there
as Uncle Jack rambled through the afternoon
recalling his days as a club boxer
when he was "Killer Cain" in an emerald robe
and he dazzled them with footwork.
Once he sparred with Willie Pep,
said he never saw the jabs, a hundred, maybe more,
but could hear the dull popping of leather,
feel them banging inside his head,
could taste them when he swallowed blood.

Sometimes between rounds he'd notice me,
crouch forward in his chair, roll his shoulders
and tuck his chin, throw a playful punch,
ask, "How much you weigh, kid?"
I'd duck down into my Coke, redfaced and grinning,
hide under their haze of cigarettes and beer
as Uncle Jack saw Willie Pep through the years,
remembered popping leather and the taste of blood.
And always the groggy refrain,
"How much you weigh, kid?"
even to my mother, looking girlish and flustered,
trying to catch my father with a glance.

"How much you weigh, kid?"
That slurred riddle rang
like a bully's jeering taunt
even after I'd taken my father's chair
until once in mid-week I discovered him —

the soft voice, the easy smile.
He told me the time he was fifteen
and he'd sneak into the fights at St. Stephen's
to watch the Pollacks and Micks
pound faith into the Protestants and Jews.
He remembered the ringed fingers of the Monsignor
squeezing his shoulder, still heard the question,
"How much you weigh, kid?"
the question leading him down to the locker room
into the sick kid's trunks and heavy gloves,
into spending money and club fights and emerald robe
as he dazzled them with footwork, toughing it out
through the Depression with sixty fights,
sparring with Willie Pep and learning
the manly art and the thick taste of blood.

My wife's friends struggle into smiles
as I rub red wine beads against my glass
into squeaking sounds, wanting these strangers
to see how that square ring shaped my uncle's life,
but when all was said and done, he was no palooka.

The silence rises between us, swollen and awkward.

Later, in a sort of apology,
I fix coffee in the kitchen,
resigned to acquaintanceship
but angry for squandering the memory,
So I tuck my chin and roll my shoulders,
shuffle footwork into a dazzling dance,
whisper pop, pop, pop-pop
to the beat of bloodsoaked gloves
drumming into the bobbing faces of my guests,
my uncle hunched and rambling at his table,
and the redfaced boy who won't be talked away.

My Father's Room

Waves of ammonia ebb
as sullen black men in whites
scrub the shrouded smell that lingered
when the lobotomy shrank you back to a child.
Lazy days of naps, spoon feedings.
Chrome rails still guard the empty bed
though you've been away two years,
leaving a face gone gray with surrender,
brittle body nurtured by tubes,
stubborn insides gurgling into plastic bags.

The bedstand contains brush, watch, rosary,
relics of habits carved from your brain.
Not knowing how to say goodbye for good
to this fearful pilgrimage site,
I lean over bedrails sorting out what's left,
remember nightmarish vigils
awkwardly trimming yellowed nails
cracked and curling like an ancient beast's,
brushing thin hair over your skull's soft place,
straining close for one parched word,
a sign, a prayer,
bashfully kissing your muted pain,
your weary eyes awaiting dark release.

Cruelly resurrected, cast into infancy
again, and then me, too, again,
two lost babies locked in limbo
while I suppressed an obscene whim:
to cradle you safely in my arms,
rock you to sleep with a lullaby,
a promise soon it would be all right,
sleep long and safe and be all right,
let me sing you sweet comfort in a lullaby,
or you, me.
You, me.

Hovey's Ice Pond: Conversation With My Grandchildren, Not Yet Born

But how did they do it?

Through the winter they harvested ice.
Man-sized saws, one man to a saw, all day long.
Horses for the big work:
clearing windfall and snow,
hitching to grapplers to pull blocks free,
dragging sledges to the icehouse shore.

An iron rail reached out from the loft.
Tongs bit into blocks.
Pulleys lifted and screeched.
Iron wheels rolled along the rail
and ice disappeared inside the dark.

Did you help them?

We could only watch from the shore.
A fence and lanterns kept off
nosy kids and dumb skaters.
If the soft spots didn't get you,
Old Man Hovey would for sure.

The pond
was a checkerboard of whites and grays.
The newest squares almost black with water.
Warning flags hung from ropes big as your arm.

I remember the men.
Blue watch caps, hunting jackets, flannel shirts.
Colors twinkling like Christmas lights
against all that winter white.

How about after winter?

Metal roofs bounced back the sun.
The cold stayed put
under sawdust blankets.
Layers of blocks up to the rafters.
Loading chutes swung down

to horsedrawn wagons.

Even when it got hot?

In the wooly days of summer,
we tracked the wagons like Indian scouts.
A trail of puddles and hooves
clanging through the neighborhood.
We pestered around the wagon
til the driver opened the oilskin tarp,
chopped us off a chunk.

Our hands were like frozen fire.
Ice slivers tingled our teeth.
And our cheeks huffed and puffed
frosty breaths into summertime.

Really? It sounds like magic. Was it magic?

Not the way you think. Not then. Only
the way things were done, had been done.
They didn't waste things, is all,
not even winter, and I was just a kid.

But it seems like magic to me now.
Especially the horses.
The iceman, ragman, Freihofer Bakeryman —
those were the last horses on city streets.
That was a kind of magic,
the way they disappeared
so fast and so forever
like a dream you don't dare trust.

Some things don't get to be magic
til after they're good and gone.
The way the iceman once,
on a forgettable summer day,
lifted the tarpaulin shroud
and brought winter back alive,
the pure wonder
of even the hardest season.

This is our secret story til I'm gone.
Then tell your mother. Your father.
Listen to what they say.

(for Beth, 14, Brian, 10)

25

"Nearby, amid lakes and battlegrounds famous in song and story, are Saratoga Springs, Fort Edward, Hudson Falls and Ticonderoga . . . Glens Falls' children are never far from nature. Almost at their doorsteps are farms, orchards, mountains and lakes—perfect country for a health-building outdoor life."

— LOOK, April 4, 1944

Bumper Hopping And The Transmigration Of Souls

Half dizzy with the weather and the dare,
we turned our backs on the granite walls,
the grim obligations
of school and nuns and God,
hotfooting it down the alley
like three infidels on fire,
skiddering the corner at O'Reilly's Pub
into the refuge of the storm.

Six blocks in that blizzard
seemed a world and a half away.
To camouflage our dark intent,
we did jumping jacks on our backs —
schoolboys sculpting angels in the snow.

Abominably white,
we waited for humpbacked cars
to trudge down the road.
Then over the snowbanks we dove,
tumbling down and keeping low
to jostle for the bumper
like scrabbling crabs
until speed held us fast
in a gutwrenching slide.

History was suddenly right in our hands —
the fatassed bumpers of Lincolns,
Hudsons, Cadillacs, DeSotos.
Disputations of Science and Faith
were as real as a busted knee:
the mutability of rock salt and ice;
the treachery of powder before it's packed;
heat rising from the foul abyss
to steam from waffled manhole covers,
sudden and cruel at breakneck speed.

Seduced by the glory of hellbent deeds,
we swapped alibis and practiced lies.
The wind snapped snow in our faces

like white-hot flames, ecstasy
thrumming through thick rubber boots
until it fiddled inside our bones
and sang through our skins,
the bright fury of the storm
hurtling past
to fill the places we had been,
piling high upon its downcast self
like the specter of undreamed of sins.

Rat Town

In Rat Town, years ago,
our fathers whispered secrets,
charms hung on frosted breaths:
swing the rifle up and out,
shoulder hugging the stock
til it grazes your cheek
like the wind.
Gentle the sight high on the ribs;
there, that's the heart.
Now squeeze,
easy, smooth as sun
easing behind the pines.

Afterward,
we studied rat death,
ruffled sleek fur,
itching to find the intimacy
an efficient bullet brings.

Now we come back to Rat Town,
park at the edge of the rich stench,
shivering against the cold.
The girls we bring
have secrets of their own,
and these must be discovered, too.
Lips touch, light as wind,
whispers turn to smoke
rising with the old sharp hope,
the glory of bright red wounds.

January Crossing, Lake Champlain

Look now how mortals are blaming the gods, for they say that evils come from us, but in fact they themselves have woes beyond their share because of their own follies.

— The Odyssey

I

The procession of horses, timber, and men
slogs down the logging road
toward the blue light of the Champlain.
Husky shouts begin a noisy halting:
reins snap, slap haunches, ribs;
cleated hooves stomp for purchase in the snow;
chains clank, jangle, click;
the load settles in its tracks with a groan.
A horse nickers, the sound like pebbles
skipping over the whiteness,
then it is gone.

Necks bowed, eyes shut to the wind,
horses lean lazily into harness,
the ornery weight of Vermont pine
nagging muscle and bone.
Men shuffle from the shore,
foot by foot hammering reckoning rods,
wonder if luck and ice will hold the hour
to the mills on the Ticonderoga side
where smokestacks fill the heavy sky.

Men fuss at hames and leather collars,
work slip-knot chains around each horse's neck,
rub grease through every link
to shun the slightest freezing.

II

The first godawful crackling
stiffens men's spines,
flashes into their hands, their heads.
Before the echo can bounce from the shore,
whippletrees are unhitched —
the skid stands free.

All is suddenly, softly, still.

A hoof cracks through the ice like a shot,
then hoof after hoof exploding,
horses slammed to their knees
in a tangle of harness and reins,
a nightmare of brutal genuflections
that disappears in a crash, a splash.
Men circle wide,
yank slip-knot chains choking tight
to make the last breath last
before the cramping of bellies and lungs.

Legs churn, clumsy with iron and bone,
the struggle to mount the crumbling ledge
a mockery of their fiercest mating —
necks stretch up from the cold,
eyes bulging with need and dread;
nostrils flare wild and red;
forelegs rise and clatter and fall,
great square teeth gnashing
foam, blood, air.

III

Soon the job is wasted.
Men slacken chains,
save what rigging they can
before the slow sinking begins:
the graceful streaming of manes and tails,
winter coats darkening like shrouds,
the slumbrous rolling onto their sides,
the long glide down through the dark,
unearthly graves.

Under sky grey as soaked ice,
men shrug off the question
in each others' eyes.
Then turn their backs on luck,
listen to the strains of hard weather —
boots crunching on crusted snow,
the moan of branches in the wind,
the grinding of their jaws,
the thundering in their chests
that will hurt all the way home.

Fresh Air Kids

The Fresh Air Fund was founded to alleviate the desperate poverty and despair of New York City's slum children . . . The Fund believes that maximum benefits derive from activities which relate children directly to woods, water, fields, plants, and animals . . . Perhaps . . . the continued success of the program lies in the fact that human nature has not changed very much in the last century.   — The Conservationist

August,
and the freeform days
rounded an uphill bend,
left us shuffling through hours
of nothing new to do.

In whispers, the rumor of Fresh Air Kids
shivered along the Adirondack town
until it haunted our hillbilly lives:
gangs of city-tough hoods
stalking hometown streets,
terrible with tattoos and black leather,
brass knuckles and switchblades
ready for blood.

In secret forts we vowed to defend
every mountain and river and field.
Around campfires, we strutted
our fluttering courage,
spit and pissed and swore
like drunken goddam solidiers.
We honed our fury
to the singing sound of whetstones
rubbing jackknives to a killing edge,
the thunk of hatchets sunk into soft bellies
of watermelons, pumpkins,
a bursting and splattering
luscious as dreams of coming glory.

And we never found a single sneering one.

Our rage lingered awhile,
turned fragile as Indian summer.
Then vanished into onrushing days
like a mirage on a shimmering road.

Who can forget the hate that thrilled us?
Or fathom the joy of bloodthirsty love?
Who can suppose what dark delights
lie still in our ignorant hearts?

Halfway Brook

WHAT WE KNEW

Before
fire burned the icehouse down,
we dabbled away summer days at Hovey's Pond.
Feet dangling from makeshift rafts,
dawdling after pickerel and bass.

And when the nights sweltered,
we raided the loft of the weighing dock.
Whooped down the loading chute
on sleek blocks of ice
that bucked and bobbed
in the rollicking waves.

WHAT WE DIDN'T KNOW

Before
it was Hovey's Pond,
at the turn of the century
a brickyard stood at the northern end.

Men made a living from earth and fire.
Boots sunk into the banks of Halfway Brook
as men slung spongy slop onto wagons,
raked the muddy load to dry in the sun.

When kilns fired the clay blood-red,
the night glowed. Sparks rose,
twirling ghosts
that waltzed across the water.

* * * * * *

Before
it was Brickyard Pond,
it was good-for-nothing
marsh on Walter Briggs' farm.
When The Revolution was won,
he took a notion into his hands
and built a dam across Halfway Brook.
The lowland acres flooded and filled,

and water powered the first grist mill
within twenty American miles.

* * * * * *

Before
it was Briggs' Pond,
war dragged on through the summer of '83.
Dispatches from northern forts warned
the men had got home in their heads.

The Commander of the Armies hurried
to secure the Canadian Front. In August,
he rode the perimeter of The Outpost at Halfway Brook.
From the fort, drums were muffled by the heat.

The general stopped at a clearing
where a farmer plowed a sloping field.
The hills rolled gentle as home in Virginia.
He dismounted. Leaned back on the lathered flank
of his white horse. Dug boots into dark soil.
Closed his eyes. Tried to remember
a time when fresh-turned earth
meant something more than unmarked graves.

* * * * * *

The farmer knew nothing of soldiering.
But he knew of the brooding man
who stood alone in the sun.
Briggs hobbled the team,
lugged a wooden bucket across the field.
Without a word,
he offered cool water from a tin cup
.as if to consecrate
the moment's peace
and the endless fighting
and dying, eight years of men dying
in the general's dark eyes.

* * * * * *

Before
Washington commanded Colonial troops,

British and French armies battled
for no man's land between wilderness forts.
On a July morning, a British escort halted
supply wagons to rest and water the oxen.
Teamsters' wives watched over children
splashing in the brook. From the woods,
Montcalm's Canadians and Indians circled,
swooped down like hungry hawks.

When the scouting party arrived from the fort,
hundreds of oxen lay slaughtered
among the scalped and mangled dead.
Melting chocolate and barrels of rum
oozed into pools of blood,
the stench unbearable in the midday sun.
For two days, they gathered bodies
scattered from Blind Rock to the marshy reeds.
One hundred sixty men, twelve women and children
buried in a common grave beside Bloody Brook.

* * * * * *

Before
The French and Indian War
made a killing ground of the road
between Ft. Ticonderoga and Ft. Edward,
Indian trails wound through uncut forest.

Mohawk, Iroquois, Mohican, Delaware —
the tribes made the day's portage
along The Great Carrying Place
to the brook halfway between the waters
of the Hudson and Lake George.

When there was peace,
they traded furs, hardened pots on open fires.
When there was war,
the trails made an easy ambush.
At dawn, captives were led to Blind Rock
where the ceremony of pain would outlast the day.
Tortured screams and burning flesh
carried for miles in the mountain air.

* * * * * *

WHAT DID _WE_ KNOW?

All over town,
soldiers were coming home
to parades
and a world made safe for democracy.
Mills hummed up and down the Hudson.
In shiny new cars, our fathers rode
into peace and prosperity.
Mothers marveled at
the magic of Hoovers and Frigidaires.
Babies arrived in droves on every block.

Our lives seemed endless,
the sunblessed hours
of long summer days.
More patient than winter,
The Cold War waited
our turn
to come out and play.

IN REMEMBRANCE:

Cpl. Robert O. Barry, U.S. Marines
Cpl. James J. Bates, U.S. Marines
Cpl. Joseph E. Brunelle, Jr., U.S. Marines
Cpl. John Pezzulo, U.S. Army

On Hearing How Water Stays In My Poems

I suppose
it's true, though I never intended. My growing up
a litany of rivers, lakes, brooks, ponds.
Summers.
Haviland's Cove, the Hudson bending above the falls.
Or the quarry at East Field. Or Glen Lake, Round Pond.
Or the gigantic slide towering at Sunnyside.
Winters.
Crockwell Pond, Crandall Park, Hovey's Ice Pond.
Later, all over Lake George
with cars, boats, motorcycles, girls.
Battleground Park, Million Dollar Beach, Shepard's Park.
Up the western shore
to Hearthstone, Diamond Point, Silver Bay,
Rogers Rock, Indian Kettles, Ticonderoga.
Down
the wilderness side: Gull Bay, Huletts Landing,
Paradise Bay, Pilot Knob, Kattskill Bay, Sandy Bay.
Memory
just naturally flows. Saying those places brings back
a stream of boyhood faces,
voices
calling nicknames
we hold onto like magic charms:
Monk, Skunk, Scorpion, Bat,
Red Dog, Curve Ball, Boo Bardot,
Tarzan, Packer, T.H.E.,
Head Man, Foot, Boom-Boom, Blade,
Weed, Snake, Croak, Swamp.
Water. Memory.
The truth, I suppose. Places. Faces.
Names
I want to cup in my hands,
offer up to the common world
we took for granted, ordinary lives
so unforgotten
they might just as well been blessed.

John Wayne, Freddy Freihofer, And The Buckskin Mare

Time is the rider that breaks youth.
— George Herbert

1.

Think of it: back when
I was a rootin tootin son-of-a-gun,
the Freihofer Bakery horses made their rounds
as regular as grandparents at holiday meals.
Down Charles Street the big gray lumbered
at high noon every Monday, Wednesday, and Saturday.
My mother hung the yellow card in the window
and I'd wait for the happy clopping of hooves,
a wagonload of doughnuts, raisin bread, pecan rings,
the best chocolate chips in any kid's world.

After the war, Uncle Leon lucked into the job
until the day he threw an epileptic fit,
flailing against the racks in a wicked spell.
The horse, my mother swears, trotted him
straight back to the barn on Albany Street
where they found him twitching and senseless
— Sweet Jesus, Mary, and Joseph —
under an avalanche of pastries and rolls.

2.

One time on my birthday,
on the Freddy Freihofer Show on TV,
on the squiggle board in front of friends forgotten now,
Big Jim Fisk waved that huge felt pen
and squiggled my cockeyed lines into . . .
the galloping grace of a paint horse,
mane and tail whipping in a wind he made me see.
Seven years old, and I watched that magic pen
reach into my buckaroo dreams and lift me
onto the back of the only wish worth waiting for.

3.

You can stable a dream for years
if it's curried and tended,

until a six acre Adirondack farm
spreads like open range in The Lone Star State.
And a haybellied mare has a maverick streak
if you've waited for twenty years.
Oh, I was a lusty John Wayne, I was,
sliding bareback on that buckskin mare,
legs squeezing her barrel flanks,
the slow ache in a boy bursting
above the hills above the Hudson,
rocking for hours in that lovemaking lope
and lather lush as September rain.

4.

Almost forty now,
all those cowboy days to dream backward to:
the farmhouse with porches and dogs underfoot,
the tack room musk of leather and sweat,
and the hills and the hay and the barn.

And one dream too many times
hurrying me home to the buckskin mare
not wintered or watered for years.
I charge down the slope toward her,
the bucket sloshing my legs, my boots.
She starts up from the bottom of the hill,
all withers and haunches and ribs,
stark as a carcass.

Her beastly pain breaks somewhere inside me,
her struggle as she keeps coming on,
heavyhoofed and heaving,
her head bowed to the bucket, drawing deep.
And I am there for her, and not too late,
and I am, at last, forgiven.
No. More than only that —

Say it, Pilgrim.

Blessed. Yes.
Saved.

After The Bad News

Your mind hammers
against sleep.
You discover habits,
follow behind them
like chains.

Whatever you set down
falls
at least once.
Elbows and knees are mad
for corners.
Doorways shrink, crowd your
heavy bones.

Your heart
numbs and flutters.
You are alone in the dark
with the early prayers:
oh god, please god,
oh mommy.

You feel each moment
start, then start
to unravel.
Just what you deserve.

The Time Being

Time, the devourer of all things.
                              —Ovid

lies by the shallows
of stagnant dreams,
curls a satisfied smile
around its unwriggling mouthful,
severs the staring head
with precise nibbles
and little licks,
rips fur from flesh
in a slow tearing sound.

He knows carrion is his to keep
and casually drop within his reach
to pause and pick each speckled bit
from mottled chest and claws,
and does not offer thanks
for his providential feast,
for such as he will have their fill
though they crawl on paralyzed paws.

Why I Hate Fenimore Cooper And Don't Go To Church, Religiously

Said to be "the most unique concrete spiral stairway in America," it permitted visitors to see the hiding place known around the world from James Fenimore Cooper's The Last of the Mohicans... *When the bridge was rebuilt in 1961, the crumbling spiral stairway was not replaced.*
   — BRIDGING THE YEARS: GLENS FALLS, NEW YORK, 1763-1978

Look at the perversity of the water... First it runs smoothly, as if meaning to go down the descent as things were ordered; then it angles about and faces the shores ... as if, having broke loose from order, it would try its hand at everything.
   — THE LAST OF THE MOHICANS
Description from the island at "Glenn's Falls"

In those days, before
common sense and the new bridge
did away with it, a stairway soared
from the island's jagged ridge.
An iron railing wound around and down
to the middle of the Hudson at the end of town.

Once, the nuns shepherded our restless flock
along Warren Street, "All-eyes-forward!"
past O'Reilly's Pub at the end of the block.
Then we marched down the hill toward
Cooper's Cave. For weeks, we'd suffered through
Local History and The Leatherstocking Tales,
spelled "Chingachgook" and "Colonel Glenn's Falls"
til our tongues turned blue
and Hometown Pride swelled like billowed sails.

It was High Adventure out in the open air,
a rare escape from our parochial school:
the world of Hawkeye, the Deer Slayer;
Magua, the Savage; Gamut, the Singing Fool.
We took as gospel what the nuns and Mr. Cooper said.
Visions of tomahawks and musket balls danced in our heads.

The relics we discovered there
drove the nuns into red-faced rage,
spun our dizzy retreat up winding stairs.
Girlie magazines, yellow with stains and age.

Beer cans balanced in a pyramid stack.
Wrinkled rubbers and Lucky Strike packs.
The words on the wall were vulgar stuff —
the devil's hand, obscenely scratched.
Stop the World, I Want to Jerk Off.
Beware: This Place Smells Like Godzilla's Snatch.

In the coming years, I began to know
what the Bible says isn't always so.
Faith and Fiction are often mistook.
And joys of the flesh are sorely needed.
What the nuns didn't know could fill a book,
and I couldn't wait to read it.

"*Typifying America as a whole, teenage boys and girls of Glens Falls . . . agree they do not know enough about their own emotions. They admit they are insufficiently instructed about sex and the meaning of marriage.*"

— *LOOK,* November 28, 1944

The *Palmer Method* Comes To A Catholic School

Round, Round, Up and Down.
The nuns spread a new kind of word,
visions of handwriting grace.
Round, Round, Up and Down.
Fountain pens circled the air,
eager for cursive flight:
a flock of F's,
a murmuration of M's,
a gaggle of G's.

Round, Round, Up and Down.
All the long year long
we practiced for perfection.
Endless rosaries of O's,
scapulars hung with H's,
T's like Calvary crosses
lined across the page.

Round, Round, Up and Down.
And when we looked up,
girls
were busting out all over
junior high
in fuzzy sweaters and tight skirts,
sashaying down the halls
to some secret rhythm
of bulges, bumps, curves.

Round, Round, Up and Down.
Boobs, Nipples, Tits, Ass.
Boobs, Nipples, Tits, Ass.
Our notebooks filled
with the wicked strokes.
Each word a caress,
forbidden wonder
smuggled into our beds.
Round, Round, Up and Down,
Boobs, Nipples, Tits, Ass,
boyflesh bursting at the seams,
prayers of love, angels
writhing through mortal dreams.

Troubled Air

A heat wave smothers July.
Brushfires, tortured air.
The sky glares
without a trace of blue.

At night, heat
swarms into upstairs rooms,
pesters sleep like a fever.
One by one by one, the sisters
leave the restlessness of their beds.

The fan is a cool purr in the dark.
Sheets billow, float to the hardwood floor.
Damp towels under their heads, they
wriggle, stretch.

The fan swivels,
pauses
at the end of its arc,
backtracks. A voice sighs, rises
and falls with the first caress:
"Aaaaaa,"
as a nightshirt puffs,
a taut rippling
at the curve of hips, breasts.
And the whirling whirr moves on,
another, softer
"Aaaaaa,"
as downy hair ruffles
legs and belly and arms, a shiver
blossoming in the blood.
A third voice quivers, a child's giddy
"Aaaaaa,"
the tintinnabulating joy
of goosebumps and funny bones,

and the fan swerves,
pauses,
shudders. The waiting
swells inside them like a wish.
The wind swings back, its girlish course
the timely flow of seasons:

"Aaaaaa,"
like a gentle breath;
"Aaaaaa,"
like a gentle breath of a boy;
"Aaaaaa,"
like a breathless touch of a gentle, breathless boy.

Going Steady, The First Time

Like Adam and Eve
awakening
in the glow of Paradise.
You, only you.
The very wonder
of each other.

Alone together, you invent
the world. Shy delight
in every plain moment,
whispers and glances
a language all your own.

As if the gods conspired
to bless your loneliness.
The sadness of sad songs,
words you know by heart.
Lovely sorrow
of the last slow dance
and bittersweet goodbyes.

In the name of love,
you remember forever:
mortal passion
stronger than hellfire,
promises
you made in the dark.
Hearts too tender,
you thought, to break.

Catholic Girls

Mortal sin was no laughing matter,
God knows,
so I believed
sex was serious,
humorless as the Catholic girls
in the dark afterward
who hurried into tangled clothes
like startled butterflies fleeing
back inside cocoons,
gathering guilt
with each lacy, silken layer,
retreating with furious regret
into silence
ringing with forsworn oaths
and catechismed vows:
and me the Judas thief
taking pleasures that they offered
but were not theirs to give.

Aunt Sara On Valentine's Night

On the stooped back of February,
she clenches legs and arms
tight around her emptiness,
lopsiding the couch
as plastic asters scratch
mad runes into the wintered pane.

Uncoiling, stiffly, she sinks
to the floor on hands and knees,
scrabbling against the hardwood grain,
one arm cradling hanging breasts
snug against the flannel robe.

Elbows framed along the peeling sill,
she presses her lips against the glass
in a cautious, frosted kiss,
savors the chill of melting ice
sliding smooth and slick,
then moved by a memory,
she traces tonguetied lines
into twin black hearts.
Lick Lick. Lick. Lick.

Aunt Sara And The Tattoo

His fingers send a skittering
along the softness of her thighs.
Her quickening swells into blue cords
bulging at his wrist, veins
coiling up his arm like snakes
to ripple red-lettered skin:
Evaline.

Her lips move over the name, taste
the bright remnant of his loving,
the awful burning of his passion
in proud flesh: *Evaline.*

She closes her eyes and finds a memory,
feels a ghostly comprehension —
    something brave and dreadful in his life,
    something gorgeous in his offering —
like the brilliant, telltale stain
of her first and unforgotten blood.

Aunt Sara And The 4-Letter Word

His voice catches at the sound,
then words and words stumbling
beyond the keen edge of regret.
But already the awful truth of it
lies between them like a knife.
She turns away, cold surprise
trying to forgive the sadness
he tries to keep from his eyes.

Home. Such a soft little word
to crush
the enormous wonder of their love.

A houseful of strangers
hover around the bed.
Her heart spins,
the room suddenly changed
as a place she's never been,
the last lovely loving hours
fading
with the long shadows of dusk
and his leaving.

His hand caresses her shoulder
with a tenderness she's never known.
Inside the unspeakable silence,
she feels the ache darkening
like a bruise around a broken bone.

Aunt Sara And The Birthday Party

Aunt Sara cackles and swoops,
and a flock of nieces and nephews scatters.
She straddles their wriggling hips,
pins babyfat arms to the floor.

With a wickedwitch grin,
she shakes and shakes her ruffled curls,
a thousand pinpoint prickles
itching into their faces,
the mad rush of ticklish giggles,
gurglings smothered and lost
in the storm of her hair.

At night she lies unsleeping,
cuddles with secrets and the dark,
twists taffy-colored strands
into girlish braids,
brushes each strand along her cheeks, her lips,
nuzzling all her unmothered babies,
the fresh of children in her hair.

What Heathens Do During Midnight Mass

Fifteen years later I still give thanks
for your wise gift one Christmas Eve when
sweat bubbled on our tingling skin,
oozed into carpet that tickled and burned
as we played on the edge of passion, and sin.
We were all lips and tongues
when a tabernacled guilt unlocked in me,
Mea Culpa whispering soft and secret
from musty altared faith,
your woman smell mingling in memory with incense,
the tight-throated fumes of melting candle wax,
and the sticky sweetness of early morning wine.

Fifteen years ago, remember?
Beneath my parents' wedding picture on the mantle,
beneath Christmas cards and candles and cuckoo clock,
we squirmed sweetly together,
damp and warm in front of flames
that hissed and spit at our gleaming skin,
hellishly warm,
heavenly warm,
squirming sweetly together
when staccato cuckoos cursed above our heads,
yanked me to my feet, chilled with dread,
my nakedness a shivering shame.

The silence echoed black inside me,
contrition throbbed through every throbbing pulse,
the silence a sore and aching thing
until you nudged it with your purling giggle,
a woman's giggle, deep and gurgling,
your breasts jiggling to the sound of giggles
tumbling over giggles with glee and gladness
and something else I barely heard —
an unheavenly grace,
a gentle benediction
that drew me down next to your goodness,
drew me down, hushed and warm
inside your arms floating up and circling round,
held me safe in your giggling mirth
in communion and salvation
like a musky angel come to earth.

The Graduate Student Learns,
In Spite Of Books

The nails can be cut easily . . . Clippers may be easier than nail scissors.
There are manicure scissors with ball points.

— Dr. Benjamin Spock
BABY AND CHILD CARE

Past midnight. The day's reading
still undone. Upstairs, my wife hugs
the blessed hours between feedings,

dreams bothered by swollen breasts.
The drowsy quiet draws me away
from the blather of books about books.

Father. Mother. Daughter.
Three castaway strangers exploring
the newborn world. Today,

the terror of fingernails
scratched across eyelid and cheek.
I drift toward the baby's room,

this vigil over her sleep a whim
growing into a habit. In the night-
light's eerie glow, my wife

kneels next to the open crib.
Eyes closed, she rests her head
beside our sleeping child.

She unfolds a fist,
holds it softly to her lips.
How perfectly the tiny hand
fits her gentle teeth.

Bewley's Cafe

1.

A squall of smells
swirls through a dream of Bewley's:
Grafton Street and Dublin a thousand dreams ago.
And my throat fills, the smell of coffee fierce
under softer scents of spice and tea,
the air warm with scones, cakes, sticky buns.
Counters piled with tea aprons, tea caddies, tea towels,
aisles of bentwood chairs, frosted panels of glass,
hardwood floors like the rings of an ancient tree
scuffled down to rivers of brown,
half a century of Irish moods.

2.

The furthest room a medley of wood and glass,
the hum of voices under tinkling and clattering.
Over coffee, I write a poem of wife and home,
study chinoiserie walls of red, yellow, green,
watch the jug of cream thicken to skin.
A man approaches, smiles with snaggled teeth.
Cater-cornered, we observe
the shyness of strangers eating alone together.
Each cake he slickens with a proper butter glaze,
savors morsels with a smacking sound,
harrumphing his way through *The Irish Times*.

3.

Then:
somehow not knowing but knowing just the same,
the woman is there across from me,
somehow unscrawling my words, upsidedown.
"It will turn out lovely when you've done."
Something about her eyes,
green eyes deepening to smoke and brown,
eyes gentling every ache I would know, or write.
Her voice rises from the hush of my dream
like the keen of gulls etched in glass:
"It's very Irish, you know.
It's sad in all the wrong places."

4.

In the upstairs room,
waitresses crinkle in starched blue frocks,
serve savouries of my mother's Catholic Fridays —
poached egg on toast, salmon salad, smoked mackerel.
Windows frame a seascape of roofs,
chimneys jutting like smokestacks of dry-docked freighters.
To the north, the stone mass of Trinity College;
to the south, the bloom of St. Stephen's Green.
Below,
Grafton Street is a midway bustling.
Vendors with baby buggies stacked with fruit and flowers.
Men in sandwich boards detouring tourists.
Double-deckers lurch from the curb. Sway.
Summoned by distant vesper bells,
an expedition of nuns parts the peopled sea.

5.

At the dream's unwinding,
I am alone in Bewley's upstairs room.
Behind me, I hear the lift's slow wheeze.
The woman hands me a packet of letters.
I untie the ribbon,
discover some vague, inconsolable loss.
Time and sound and memory are suspended:
we are lost together in the eye of the storm.
And for a time inside of time,
I feel her lying against me,
hold her close, safe from night's dark dreaming,
my hand that rests along her face
a goblet filled with sleeping breaths.

6.

How to wake, then,
and shrug from bones
a dream's shivery dreaming?
How to atone for this brooding passion,
such sins, such undishonored dreams?

"If Glens Falls is a fair sample, our American young people are ambitious. Most of them dream, as youth always does, of professions or white-collar jobs."

— *LOOK*, November 28, 1944

"How many . . . will want to leave Glens Falls?"

— *LOOK*, June 27, 1944

History Lesson

1.

Father,
I couldn't forgive you that time
in your white shirt grayed with sweat,
maroon tie with blue eagles, talons
outstretched like an avenging multitude
diving toward your jangling belt.

I was sincere in booklearned truth,
a rage that was all the rage.
I'd woken to the dream of King,
the gospel of Baldwin, Cleaver,
Ellison and Malcolm —
you had to read them.

Instead,
you mopped your plate with folded bread,
gravy splotching your tie. Glowering
around obscene mouthfuls,
you growled,
"Leave the bullshit to the bulls."

2.

Daughter,
forgive me this morning
when I preached to you
the perfect pragmatism and oafish beauty
of the bucket-jawed pelicans.

You were sincere
when you explained that all
the first graders knew
the stupid pelicans go blind
from too much crashing into waves
headfirst, with their eyes open.

I thought I'd forsaken vulgar ties,
but a voice inside me
I thought I'd left behind
growled before I said it,
"Leave the bullshit to the bulls."

Salvation Army Duds

Ft. Lauderdale City Commissioners . . . proposed spraying beach-area garbage cans with kerosene to discourage vagrants from foraging through them for food.

— MIAMI HERALD

In Salvation Army duds
they slouch and shuffle
like circus bears
half untamed,
sniffing potato salad
and wrinkled hot dogs,
prowling poisoned bins

til night:
wizardry of blanket rolls
turns tables into bridges
for trolls to curl up under
dreams of hometowns left behind,
the waves a nomad's welcome
murmuring lunatic lullabyes.

The Sunshine State

FLORIDA. THE RULES ARE DIFFERENT HERE.
— 1987 promotional slogan
Florida Department of Commerce

Here the onshore breeze is a sheer
blessing. Plastic birds and dragons veer,
shudder into the sky with a colorful flair.
On the warm back of gulfstream air,
the rules of coldhearted spring
are suspended: here is no painstaking
work of kites, feet pounding
over crusted ground until they sting,
hands and cheeks blustered raw
to kindle rumors of an early thaw.

Here lies the promise of tropical ease,
a bright new world flaunting gravity's
laws. Here a lazy smugness settles in;
kites swagger above beach chairs, forgotten
as the day's sweet heat is undone
with frozen concoctions of tequila and rum.

But here, dusk smolders with a mean surprise —
skin blazing, livid as the sunstruck evening sky.
Even the soft night breeze rubs like a jagged stone,
sending fire enough to chill the deepest bones.

Stricken Testimony

Did God rage or chuckle
as the bolt left his fist?

The matter's irrelevant.
Case dismissed.

Three Hypotheses For Bearded Poets

Full of strange oaths, and bearded as the pard,/Jealous in honor,
sudden and quick in quarrel,/Seeking the bubble reputation . . .
— AS YOU LIKE IT

1.

Afraid of playing the darling boy, again,
they put their fathers' faces behind them,
disdaining generations of dimples and chins,
proud prodigal sons forsaking legacies
of ignorant uncles and fussy old aunts.

2.

Or
they wear the whiskery wisdom of Whitman,
singing songs of themselves to themselves,
constantly risking absurdity,
barking Ginsberg's hairy hairy howl.

3.

Or
at some time, in some newspaper,
bewitched by a photograph
as foolhardy, even, as poetry —
"The Year's Best Beard of Bees."
Scratching their chins,
they tingled with the ticklish itch,
the twitch of thousands of bees, stirring,
the uneasiness it brings,
knowing well that some precarious things
are more ungentle than they seem.
They sting, sweet suffering
Jesus, they sting.

Fingers, Fists, Gabriel's Wings

My voice, plucked from the air,
clasped in the interpreter's hands:
fists bloom, close,
pulse of hothouse flowers;
supple fingerpuppet dancers
move to unsounded strains.

Watching the deaf girl listen,
I think there is more to words
than sound ever knows,
brimming handfuls of speech
tempered by secondhand grace.
The word, unutterably, made flesh:
fingers flutter, hover, fold,
the whisk of Gabriel's wings.

Agnostic And Son

As I boost him onto the chair,
my students get interested — in him,
his bandaged hand, even me, teacher
turned father before their eyes.
The hand bigger than Popeye's
fist, but not funny. Under gauze
and ointment, the palm scraped
past flesh and bleeding, fingers
swollen and burst like sausages.

I go on as if he weren't there.

I could explain, but what would I say?
He's stubborn and stupid and five years old,
and the god of escalators didn't care.
But he's a good boy, trying hard
to play with the toy I let him bring.
He shifts in the chair, all his body
moving slow, the pain that rode him
through the night familiar now
in a world so awfully changed, so
wickedly strange the hand

forgets, fumbles, the wound
rubbed rough. His face tightens.
His good hand —
its name there waiting in my head —
his good hand reaches out for the bad,
cradles it, lays it down
like a precious thing. Then a deep,
filling breath, an effort to swallow
the pain. I look away, notice the girl
who turns and wipes her eyes, smudges
blotching her perfect cheeks.

Already the moment is blessed forever.
His deep breath, her quiet tears —
courage and compassion
the only sacraments I know.
The holy silence of pain,
the wordlessness of love,
the ungodly tenderness of the world.

Class Reunion

We are nigh the spot that Providence first placed them at, but where, it seems, they were too rebellious to stay . . .
— THE LAST OF THE MOHICANS
Hawkeye describing the island at "Glenn's Falls"

Hell, I'm a long way from the state of grace. I'm in New Jersey now.
— overheard at 25th Year Reunion
St. Mary's Academy, Class of '63
Queensbury Hotel, Glens Falls, NY

I.

Unmistakable belly laughs —
Jake and Boom-Boom and Skunk
roaring us back through the years,
two short blocks past convent walls
to the granite fortress of St. Mary's.

The commotion of the cocktail hour
fills the vaulted ceiling of the lobby
like half-forgotten echoes
of bag lunches and pep rallies,
assemblies in The Great Hall.

"I may be old, but I'm not grown up!"
The joke ripples across the room,
splashes of laughter
toasting a promise
hidden inside a prayer.

II.

A mural rises above the fireplace:
The Last of the Mohicans
sprawling larger than life
across the east wall of the lobby.
Cunning Hawkeye and wise Chingachgook
have rescued four misguided strangers
in the secret cave behind Glenn's Falls.

The cavern is heavy with shadows.
For the moment, they are safe
in the narrow escape, unaware
they have doomed Uncas

and cursed the Delaware tribe, forever.

Hawkeye lifts a burning pine knot
to show the way, and light flickers
on the two sisters huddled in the dark,
their dreadful need
urging the blessed and the damned
down the fateful path of Cooper's tale.

III.

We gather beneath the mural
for the reunion portrait.
How many times
have we stood this way before?

The painting frames the background
in dozens of scrapbook poses,
Hawkeye raising the torch above
the celebrations of our lives.
First Communion. Confirmation.
Award Banquets. Proms.
Weddings. Anniversaries.
The years counting off
like rosary beads, decades
disappearing under our thumbs.

IV.

However far we've come,
this need to untangle change
never changes.

Even the best of us
have a bone to pick
with the ghost of days gone by.
Familiar stories mingle with new lies.
Former lovers blush,
barely touch, smiles aching
with betrayal and regret.
Fast faders and late bloomers,
we envy the crying shame

of each others' bad luck.

The good old days
multiply like loaves and fishes,
a feast of happy endings
to that once upon a time
when everything mattered,
most things hurt.

V.

Who can say what brings us here
or what answers we're looking for?
Only this: we hold those days
in the palm of our hands
like the small wonder
of a Nativity scene
sheltered
inside a waterdome.

We shake the heavens. Snow
glitters down without a sound.
All is calm and bright.
The white hush over Bethlehem
calls us back
from the world we've come to know

where demons laugh outside the window
and darkness stalks the driven snow.

Burning Dreams On The Sun

LONG BEACH, Calif. (AP) *A truck driver with 45 weather balloons rigged to a lawn chair took a 45 minute ride . . . up to 16,000 feet before he got cold, shot some balloons with a BB gun and crashed into a power line.*

Were there too many turnaround loads,
distance measured by all-night diners,
hours yawning through too much coffee,
kidneys throbbing again at 3 a.m.?
Were there too many nights on your hands
that hung like chains from the wheel,
monotonous, humdrum motion
droning away the sound of your dream?
And did the darkness ever whisper,
it might not work, it might not,
nearly grounding you in mortal shame,
too foolish ever to dream again?

Icarus, too, must have felt like you,
restless with impudent wonder.
No labyrinth could hold him;
he flew on wings of feathers and wax
until he burned his dreams on the sun.
But no matter. For a time,
you dared to leave the darkful land,
rising high in wacky flight
like an uncouth god, purified by light.

Sun Down, Key West

(For John)

You feel the land darken behind you,
easing the rage of the dogday sun.
Dusk settles down with a sigh
as soft as *maracas* rattling
palms, and sand, and shells.

You feel the day's swansong hour
rising from Mallory Dock
on the lilt of a bamboo flute,
an artist's hand tracing
fandango rhythms of a peddler
juggling mangos and plums and limes.

You remember that long last light
hanging in clouds after it should be gone.
You remember that same old surprise —
day scattering ashes on a flamingo sky
as the sun *limbos* slowly under the sea.

Anniversary Song

We make lazy love
in the morning, now,
nuzzle sleep away
with murmuring, sighs,
hushed overture
of a nightgown
playing soft
over familiar thighs.

We know the ease
of practiced measures,
harmony joined
in rhythmic motion,
a comfortable passion
that endures
in vaguely muted
variations.

Stepfather

I swear, your mother doesn't snore. She purrs.

So time has another trick up its sleeve.
Widow weds widower.   Catholic and Jew.
Happily ever after   after
unhappy endings they've been through.

Once more we've come home to roost
at the kitchen table, four chairs left
holding up under thirty years of family.
Our baker's half dozen.   A game of
musical chairs that never stops;
we slouch against doorjambs;
perch on countertops.   All our lives
we have crowded this room with our need.
Hunger and thirst, confessions and lies,
glorious insults, uproarious laughs,
comings and goings and going nowheres.
Our mother clucking over her wayward brood,
making the best of things.   Making do.

Stepfather, stranger, thief —
we've come home to make do with you.
As if our blessing forgave you for living
in the shadow of a father's ghost.

Good man.   Gentle man.
Try to understand: we are uneasy
with your joy;   newly-wed
secrets unlocked like treasure
left behind in the marriage bed.

Jesus, Mary, and Joseph —
how many times must we learn
how much we can never know?
Tonight, unsleeping, you will turn
from our mother's purring sleep
wondering
if it was always so
or it is you who brings her such content.
And we, in strangely familiar beds,
will listen into that other darkness
remembering
all the things our father never said.

Plastic Flamingos

Necks bend double, twisted into s's
by the tug of humid days and nights and days;
one leg tangled in St. Augustine grass,
the other tucked tight, half ready for flight.
Plastic flamingos hold a dainty ache,
pink firebrands of memory,
our many northern places
where sambo stableboys, old as iron,
held hitching rings for generations
of horses that never came. Or would.

And so we humor ourselves,
flamingos in gaudy splendor
a preposterous High Kitsch joke
against the sham of Florida seasons,
the high-rises faulting from the sand
like sheer cliffs of glass
hoarding the sun and breeze,
turning a glimpse of sea
back to the sea.

And yet —
on the concrete pedestal thrust from the lawn,
the silver ornamental globe
reflects
a sudden, unaccustomed grace:
flamingos hover and curve,
the first blush
in a world gone round
and perfectly plain,
lovely as sprinklers pulsing gently
in a gentler summer rain.

"In the postwar years it will be partly the task of Glens Falls' children—and children all over America—to make better what is good, replace what is bad and fructify the future for themselves and their fellow men."

— LOOK, April 4, 1944

— E P I L O G U E —

Glens Falls: Twenty-Five Years Later

The hill seems empty now, another shrunken space,
no buildings squeezed shoulder to shoulder,
just one clean dip from the top to the bridge.
Halfway up, the new Civic Center commands the slope,
and on Saturdays, out of wind and cold,
boys named Chad and Brett and Shawn,
bulky in matching uniforms and headgear,
skim red and blue lines with Olympic strides,
slick with polished sticks and padded gloves
under the whistles of blackwhitestriped men.

When I grew here,
when the snow was light and the ice was thick,
we'd circle the island up at Crandall Pond,
leaning into turns on footlong racers
flashing like sabers in the winter sun.
Once I jumped icetrapped logs
with Snake and Boom-Boom and Kel,
dropping markers of motherknitted mittens.
I boasted down rising fear,
tearing through the stinging wind,
then crashed through icecrust like an April stone,
waist deep: frozen, dumb, surprised.
We laughed when they stripped me dry,
then shivered home together, foolish and scared,
my arms gangling out of Kel's blue parka
like a gawky Eskimo, reddening in the cold.
Legs stuffed into the arms of Snake's sweater,
I did a stepinfetchit shuffle
in goofy upsidedown pants.

When I grew here,
we raced through the frozen windfall days
in a world that was safe as a memory.
Life would get more absurd and reckless, we found,
and more chilling than we thought it could be.

75

About The Author

Michael Cleary was born in 1945, three months after *LOOK* Magazine's final installment of the "Hometown, USA" series. He grew up in Glens Falls, graduated from St. Mary's Academy, and returned from college to teach English at Queensbury High School. At the age of thirty, he left for Tennessee to earn a doctorate in English, then joined the faculty of Broward Community College in Ft. Lauderdale, Florida. He lives in Plantation with his wife, Kay (a Glens Falls native), and their two children, Beth and Brian.

AMERICAN BOOK SERIES AWARDS

Sponsored By:

SAN DIEGO POETS PRESS
Editor/Publisher: Kathleen Iddings

The Counting of Grains	by	*Joan LaBombard*	*1989*
Yarrow Field	by	*Regina McBride*	*1990*
The Only Cure I Know	by	*Charles Atkinson*	*1991*
Hometown, USA	by	*Michael Cleary*	*1992*

San Diego Poets Press is a not-for-profit organization originated in 1981 for the purpose of supporting contemporary poetry and poets, and furthering the literary arts in general. We gratefully acknowledge those who have supported our efforts:

California Arts Council

Security Pacific Bank

Danah Fayman

Howard Bernstein

Union Bank

Finch, Pruyn & Company, Inc.

Anonymous Patrons

This book is printed on
Finch Fine, VHF, Basis 70, Bright White
Finch Fine Cover, VHF, 65 lb. Bright White
Manufactured by Finch, Pruyn & Company, Inc.
Glen Falls, NY 12801

San Diego Poets Press
Editor/Publisher: Kathleen Iddings
P.O. Box 8638
La Jolla, CA 92038

For any combination of the American Book Series:

1 book:	$10.00 plus $2.00 postage/handling	$12.00
2 books:	$20.00 plus $2.00 postage/handling	$22.00
3 books:	$20.00 plus $2.00 postage/handling	$32.00
4 books:	$20.00 plus $2.00 postage/handling	$42.00

Name _____ Date _____

Address _____